BLAZERS

SUPER SPEED

ATV
Racing

BY TRACY NELSON MAURER

Reading Consultant:
Barbara J. Fox
Reading Specialist
Professor Emerita
North Carolina State University

Content Consultant:
Rick Sosebee
Off-road Powersports Journalist
Dawsonville, Georgia

CAPSTONE PRESS
a capstone imprint

Blazers Books are published by Capstone Press,
1710 Roe Crest Drive, North Mankato, Minnesota 56003
www.capstonepub.com

Library of Congress Cataloging-in-Publication Data
Cataloging-in-publication information is on file with the Library of Congress.
ISBN 978-1-4765-0119-2 (library binding)
ISBN 978-1-4765-3367-4 (eBook PDF)

Editorial Credits
Kathryn Clay and Christopher L. Harbo, editors; Gene Bentdahl, designer;
Eric Manske, production specialist

Photo Credits
Alamy: dmac, 18-19, 22-23, Michael Doolittle, 16-17, Rick Edwards ARPS, 11, Robert Grubba, 15,
Transtock Inc./David LeBon, 7; Getty Images: Francois Dubourg, 29; Harlen Foley - ATVriders.com,
20-21; Newscom: ZUMA Press, cover; Shutterstock: CTR Photos, 26, Dennis Donohue, 8-9, James
Edwards, 24-25, Mana Photo, 5, Marcel Jancovic, 12-13

Artistic Effects
Shutterstock: 1xpert, My Portfolio, rodho

Printed in the United States of America in Stevens Point, Wisconsin.
032013   007227WZF13

TABLE OF CONTENTS

ANY PLACE, ANY SEASON

Dust clouds trail behind **all-terrain** vehicles (ATVs) as they take off from the starting line. Mud sprays the ATVs as they race through wooded paths. Mud pits, **dunes**, and steep hills are no match for these powerful machines.

all-terrain—suitable for use in many different conditions

dune—a large hill of sand

FAST FACT

ATVs are also called quads or four-wheelers because of their four big tires.

BUILT TOUGH

Early ATVs had six wheels. Companies built three-wheelers in the 1980s, but these machines often rolled over. During the late 1980s, four-wheelers became popular off-road machines for riding on trails and racing.

FAST FACT

An ATV's top speed is about 80 miles (129 kilometers) per hour. In 2008 an ATV with a specially built engine reached 196 miles (315 km) per hour.

Thick tire **treads** help ATVs tackle difficult trails. Race teams switch tires for better **traction** in different conditions. Paddle tires with large treads let riders speed through dunes. Riders use studded tires on ice.

tread—a series of bumps and deep grooves on a tire

traction—the gripping power that holds a vehicle's tires to the ground

FAST FACT

Each ATV racing tire costs more than $50. A racing team might use more than eight tires during a single day of racing.

Cross-country (XC) races are held on narrow forest paths or wide-open deserts. These trails have many rocks and other hazards. ATVs used in XC races have metal skid plates on their undersides to protect parts from damage.

FAST FACT

The exhaust system hushes the loud rumble of an ATV motor. Most racetracks have rules that limit ATV engine sound to 99 decibels. That's about as loud as barking dogs in a kennel.

exhaust—the waste gases produced by an engine

PHOTO DIAGRAM

1. **EXHAUST**

2. **THROTTLE**

3. **HELMET**

4. **BRAKE**

5. **SUSPENSION**

6. **TRANSPONDER FOR RECORDING RACE TIMES**

7. **STUDDED TIRE**

8. **BOOT**

GET READY TO RACE

The length of an ATV race depends on the **class**, the type of race, and the track or course. ATV motocross (MX) races might end after 15 minutes or a certain number of laps. XC events can last more than two hours.

class—a competitive group with similar skill levels and machines

Racers of the same age or skill level race against one another in the same class. Kids can start racing at age 4 using specially sized ATVs. They must take a training course. Like all ATV racers, they also wear full safety gear.

FAST FACT

Safety gear for ATV racers includes helmets, gloves, goggles, boots, and chest protectors.

MX is the most popular ATV track racing event. Racers drive side by side on dirt tracks that are 0.5 to 1.5 miles (0.8 to 2.4 km) long. They claw through mud and jump over **whoops**.

whoops—a series of small mounds or jumps

FAST FACT

The All-Terrain Vehicle Association (ATVA) works with the American Motorcyclist Association (AMA) to set rules for ATV MX races.

FAST FACT

About 500 to 800 racers compete at each AMA national event. The motocross national final is held in early August in Hurricane Mills, Tennessee.

The largest professional and **amateur** MX series is the AMA Motocross National Championship. Racers compete in 10 to 12 races from March to August. The racer with the most points at the end of the season wins the championship.

amateur—an athlete who is not paid for taking part in a sport

During a hare scramble, racers ride about two hours in a single race. Riders need to be in good physical condition to win these long races. The AMA Hare Scrambles National Championship series includes several races around the United States each year.

ATV track races usually run timed qualifying **heats** before a main event. The fastest racers compete in the main event.

heat—one of several early races that determine which drivers advance to the main event

FAST FACT

Doug "Digger" Gust began racing at 17 years old. Today he holds many records, including the most AMA championships.

ATV racing is exciting but demanding. Throughout each race, drivers must shift their body weight. Shifting weight balances the machine so it does not roll over. Racers work out to build the strength they need to succeed.

MORE ATV ACTION AHEAD

Thousands of people fill the stands to cheer for their favorite ATV racers. Every year the sport attracts new riders and promises thrills for its many loyal fans.

GLOSSARY

all-terrain (AWL-tuh-RAYN)—suitable for use in many different conditions

amateur (AM-uh-chur)—an athlete who is not paid for taking part in a sport

class (CLASS)—a competitive group with similar skill levels and machines

dune (DOON)—a large hill of sand

exhaust (ig-ZAWST)—the waste gases produced by an engine

heat (HEET)—one of several early races that determine which drivers advance to the main event

traction (TRAK-shuhn)—the gripping power that holds a vehicle's tires to the ground

tread (TRED)—a series of bumps and deep grooves on a tire

whoops (WHOOPS)—a series of small mounds or jumps

READ MORE

David, Jack. *ATVs.* Cool Rides. Minneapolis: Bellwether Media, 2008.

Peppas, Lynn. *ATVs and Off-roaders.* Vehicles on the Move. New York: Crabtree Pub., 2012.

Tieck, Sarah. *ATVs.* Amazing Vehicles. Edina, Minn.: ABDO Pub. Co., 2010.

INTERNET SITES

FactHound offers a safe, fun way to find Internet sites related to this book. All of the sites on FactHound have been researched by our staff.

Here's all you do:

Visit *www.facthound.com*

Type in this code: 9781476501192

 Check out projects, games and lots more at
www.capstonekids.com

31

INDEX